Who Am I?

by

Sri Ramana Maharshi

Sai ePublications

All rights reserved. No part of this material may be reproduced or transmitted in any form, or by any means electronic or mechanical, including photocopy, recording, or by any information storage and retrieval system without the written permission of the publisher, except for inclusion of brief quotations in a review.

— Publisher

Who Am I?

By Sri Ramana Maharshi

Published by: Sai ePublications

ISBN-13: 9781537599212

Contents

Introduction 1

Who Am I? 7

Introduction

Who am I? is the title given to a set of questions and answers bearing on Self-enquiry. The questions were put to Bhagavan Sri Ramana Maharshi by Sri M. Sivaprakasam Pillai, about the year 1902. Sri Pillai, a graduate in philosophy, was at the time employed in the Revenue Department of the South Arcot Collectorate. During his visit to Tiruvannamalai in 1902 on official work, he went to Virupaksha Cave on Arunachala Hill and met the Maharshi there. He sought from him spiritual guidance and solicited answers to questions relating to Self-enquiry. As Bhagavan was not talking then, not because of any vow he had taken but because he did not have the inclination to talk, he answered questions put to him by writing. As recollected and recorded by Sri Sivaprakasam Pillai, there were thirteen questions and answers to them given by Bhagavan. This record was first published by Sri Pillai in 1923 (in the original Tamil), along with a couple of poems composed by himself relating how Bhagavan's grace operated in his case by dispelling his doubts and by saving him from a crisis in life.

Who am I? has been published several times subsequently. We find thirteen questions and answers in some editions and twenty-eight in others. There is also another published version in which the questions are not given, and the teachings are rearranged in the form of an essay. The extant English translation is of this essay. The present rendering is of the text in the form of twenty-eight questions and answers.

Along with *Vicharasangraham* (Self-Enquiry), *Nan Yar* (Who am I?) constitutes the first set of instructions in the Master's own words. These two are the only prose pieces among Bhagavan's works. They clearly set forth the central teaching that the direct path to liberation is Self-enquiry. The particular mode in which the enquiry is to be made is lucidly set forth in *Nan Yar*. The mind consists of thoughts. The "I"-thought is the first to arise in the mind. When the enquiry "Who am I?" is persistently pursued, all other thoughts get destroyed, and finally the "I"-thought itself vanishes leaving the supreme non-dual Self alone. The false identification of the Self with the phenomena of non-self such as the body and mind, thus ends, and there is illumination, *sakshatkara*. The process of enquiry, of course, is not an easy one. As one enquires "Who am I?", other thoughts will arise; but as these arise, one should not yield to them by following them; on the contrary, one should ask, "To whom do they arise?" In order to do this, one has to be extremely vigilant. Through constant enquiry one should make the mind stay in its source, without allowing it to wander away and get lost in the mazes of thought created by itself. All other disciplines such as breath-control and meditation on the forms of God should be regarded as auxiliary practices. They are useful so far as they help the mind to become quiescent and one-pointed. For the mind that has gained skill in concentration Self-enquiry becomes comparatively easy. It is by ceaseless enquiry that the thoughts are destroyed and the Self realised – the plenary Reality in which there is not even the "I"-thought, the experience which is referred to as "Silence".

This, in substance, is Bhagavan Sri Ramana Maharshi's teachings in *Nan Yar* (Who am I?).

T.M.P. Mahadevan
University of Madras
June 30, 1982

Bhagavan Sri Ramana Maharshi
(At the age of 21)

Who Am I?

Nan Yar

All living beings desire to be happy always, without any misery. In everyone there is observed supreme love for oneself. And happiness alone is the cause of love. In order therefore, to gain that happiness which is one's nature and which is experienced in the state of deep sleep, where there is no mind, one should know oneself. To achieve this, the Path of Knowledge, the enquiry in the form of "Who am I?", is the principal means.

1. *Who am I?*

The gross body which is composed of the seven humours (*dhatus*), I am not; the five cognitive sense organs, viz., the senses of hearing, touch, sight, taste and smell, which apprehend their respective objects, viz. sound, touch, colour, taste and odour, I am not; the five cognative sense organs, viz., the organs of speech, locomotion, grasping, excretion and procreation, which have as their respective functions, speaking, moving, grasping, excreting and enjoying, I am not; the five vital airs, *prana*, etc., which perform respectively the five functions of in-breathing, etc., I am not; even the mind which thinks, I am not; the nescience too, which is endowed only with the residual impressions of objects and in which there are no objects and no functionings, I am not.

2. *If I am none of these, then who am I?*

After negating all of the above mentioned as 'not this', 'not this', that Awareness which alone remains – that I am.

3. *What is the nature of Awareness?*

The nature of Awareness is Existence-Consciousness-Bliss.

4. When will the realization of the Self be gained?

When the world which is what-is-seen has been removed, there will be realization of the Self which is the seer.

5. Will there not be realization of the Self even while the world is there (taken as real)?

There will not be.

6. Why?

The seer and the object seen are like the rope and the snake. Just as the knowledge of the rope which is the substratum will not arise unless the false knowledge of the illusory serpent goes, so the realization of the Self which is the substratum will not be gained unless the belief that the world is real is removed.

7. When will the world which is the object seen be removed?

When the mind, which is the cause of all cognition and of all actions, becomes quiescent, the world will disappear.

8. What is the nature of the mind?

What is called 'mind' is a wondrous power residing in the Self. It causes all thoughts to arise. Apart from thoughts, there is no such thing as mind. Therefore, thought is the nature of mind. Apart from thoughts, there is no independent entity called the world. In deep sleep there are no thoughts, and there is no world. In the states of waking and dream, there are thoughts, and there is a world also. Just as the spider emits the thread (of the web) out of itself and again withdraws it into itself, likewise the mind projects the world out of itself and again resolves it into itself. When the mind comes out of the Self, the world appears. Therefore, when the world appears (to be real), the Self does not appear; and when the Self appears (shines) the world does not appear. When one persistently inquires into the nature of the mind, the mind will end leaving the Self (as the residue). What is referred to as the Self is the *Atman*. The mind always exists only in dependence on something gross; it cannot stay alone. It is the mind that is called the subtle body or the soul (*jiva*).

9. What is the path of inquiry for understanding the nature of the mind?

That which rises as 'I' in this body is the mind. If one inquires as to where in the body the thought 'I' rises first, one would discover that it rises in the heart. That is the place of the mind's origin. Even if one thinks constantly 'I-I', one will be led to that place. Of all the thoughts that arise in the mind, the 'I'-thought is the first. It is only after the rise of this that the other thoughts arise. It is after the appearance of the first personal pronoun that the second and third personal pronouns appear; without the first personal pronoun there will not be the second and third.

10. *How will the mind become quiescent?*

By the inquiry 'Who am I?'. The thought 'Who am I?' will destroy all other thoughts, and like the stick used for stirring the burning pyre, it will itself in the end get destroyed. Then, there will arise Self-realization.

11. *What is the means for constantly holding on to the thought 'Who am I?'*

When other thoughts arise, one should not pursue them, but should inquire: 'To whom do they arise?' It does not matter how many thoughts arise. As each thought arises, one should inquire with diligence, 'To whom has this thought arisen?'. The answer that would emerge would be 'to me'. Thereupon if one inquires 'Who am I?', the mind will go back to its source; and the thought that arose will become quiescent. With repeated practice in this manner, the mind will develop the skill to stay in its source. When the mind that is subtle goes out through the brain and the sense-organs, the gross names and forms appear; when it stays in the heart, the names and forms disappear. Not letting the mind go out, but retaining it in the Heart is what is called 'inwardness' (*antarmukha*). Letting the mind go out of the Heart is known as 'externalisation' (*bahirmukha*). Thus, when the mind stays in the Heart, the 'I' which is the source of all thoughts will go, and the Self which ever exists will shine. Whatever one does, one should do without the egoity 'I'. If one acts in that way, all will appear as of the nature of Siva (God).

12. *Are there no other means for making the mind quiescent?*

Other than inquiry, there are no adequate means. If through other means it is sought to control the mind, the mind will appear to be controlled, but will again go forth. Through the control of breath also, the mind will become quiescent; but it will be quiescent only so long as the breath remains controlled, and when the breath resumes the mind also will again start moving and will wander as impelled by residual impressions. The source is the same for both mind and breath. Thought, indeed, is the nature of the mind. The thought 'I' is the first thought of the mind; and that is egoity. It is from that whence egoity originates that breath also originates. Therefore, when the mind becomes quiescent, the breath is controlled, and when the breath is controlled the mind becomes quiescent. But in deep sleep, although the mind becomes quiescent, the breath does not stop. This is because of the will of God, so that the body may be preserved and other people may not be under the impression that it is dead. In the state of waking and in *samadhi*, when the mind becomes quiescent the breath is controlled. Breath is the gross form of mind. Till the time of death, the mind keeps breath in the body; and when the body dies, the mind takes the breath along with it. Therefore, the exercise of breath control is only an aid for rendering the mind quiescent (*manonigraha*); it will not destroy the mind (*manonasa*).

Like the practice of breath control, meditation on the forms of God, repetition of *mantras*, restriction on food, etc., are but aids for rendering the mind quiescent.

Through meditation on the forms of God and through repetition of *mantras*, the mind becomes one-pointed. The mind will always be wandering. Just as when a chain is given to an elephant to hold in its trunk it will go along grasping the chain and nothing else, so also when the mind is occupied with a name or form it will grasp that alone. When the mind expands in the form of countless thoughts, each thought becomes weak; but as thoughts get resolved the mind becomes one-pointed and strong; for such a mind Self-inquiry will become easy. Of all the restrictive rules, that relating to the taking of *sattvic* food in moderate quantities is the best; by observing this rule, the *sattvic* quality of mind will increase, and that will be helpful to Self-inquiry.

13. The residual impressions (thoughts) of objects appear unending like the waves of an ocean. When will all of them get destroyed?

As the meditation on the Self rises higher and higher, the thoughts will get destroyed.

14. Is it possible for the residual impressions of objects that come from beginningless time, as it were, to be

resolved, and for one to remain as the pure Self?

Without yielding to the doubt 'Is it possible, or not?', one should persistently hold on to the meditation on the Self. Even if one be a great sinner, one should not worry and weep 'O! I am a sinner, how can I be saved?' One should completely renounce the thought 'I am a sinner' and concentrate keenly on meditation on the Self; then, one would surely succeed. There are not two minds – one good and the other evil; the mind is only one. It is the residual impressions that are of two kinds – auspicious and inauspicious. When the mind is under the influence of auspicious impressions it is called good; and when it is under the influence of inauspicious impressions it is regarded as evil.

The mind should not be allowed to wander towards worldly objects and what concerns other people. However bad other people may be, one should bear no hatred for them. Both desire and hatred should be eschewed. All that one gives to others one gives to one's self. If this truth is understood who will not give to others? When one's self arises all arises; when one's self becomes quiescent all becomes quiescent. To the extent we behave with humility, to that extent there will result good. If the mind is rendered quiescent, one may live anywhere.

15. How long should inquiry be practised?

As long as there are impressions of objects in the mind, so long the inquiry 'Who am I?' is required. As thoughts arise they should be destroyed then and there in the very place of their origin, through inquiry. If one resorts to contemplation of the Self unintermittently, until the Self is gained, that alone would do. As long as there are enemies within the fortress, they will continue to sally forth; if they are destroyed as they emerge, the fortress will fall into our hands.

16. What is the nature of the Self?

What exists in truth is the Self alone. The world, the individual soul and God are appearances in it, like silver in mother-of-pearl; these three appear at the same time and disappear at the same time.

The Self is that where there is absolutely no 'I'-thought. That is called 'Silence'. The Self itself is the world; the Self itself is 'I'; the Self itself is God; all is Siva, the Self.

17. *Is not everything the work of God?*

Without desire, resolve, or effort, the sun rises; and in its mere presence, the sun-stone emits fire, the lotus blooms, water evaporates, people perform their various functions and then rest. Just as in the presence of the magnet the needle moves, it is by virtue of the mere presence of God that the souls governed by the three (cosmic) functions or the fivefold divine activity perform their actions and then rest, in accordance with their respective *karmas*. God has no resolve; no *karma* attaches itself to Him. That is like worldly actions not affecting the sun, or like the merits and demerits of the other four elements not affecting all-pervading space.

18. *Of the devotees, who is the greatest?*

He who gives himself up to the Self that is God is the most excellent devotee. Giving one's self up to God means remaining constantly in the Self without giving room for the rise of any thoughts other than that of the Self.

Whatever burdens are thrown on God, He bears them. Since the supreme power of God makes all things move, why should we, without submitting ourselves to it, constantly worry ourselves with thoughts as to what should be done and how, and what should not be done and how not? We know that the train carries all loads, so after getting on it why should we carry our small luggage on our head to our discomfort, instead of putting it down in the train and feeling at ease?

19. *What is non-attachment?*

As thoughts arise, destroying them utterly without any residue in the very place of their origin is non-attachment. Just as the pearl-diver ties a stone to his waist, sinks to the bottom of the sea and there takes the pearls, so each one of us should be endowed with non-attachment, dive within oneself and obtain the Self-Pearl.

20. *Is it not possible for God and the Guru to effect the liberation of a soul?*

God and the Guru will only show the way to liberation; they will not by themselves take the soul to the state of liberation.

In truth, God and the Guru are not different. Just as the prey which has fallen into the jaws of a tiger has no escape, so those who have come within the ambit of the Guru's gracious look will be saved by the Guru and will not get lost; yet, each one should, by his own effort pursue the path shown by God or Guru and gain liberation. One can know oneself only with one's own eye of knowledge, and not with somebody else's. Does he who is Rama require the help of a mirror to know that he is Rama?

21. *Is it necessary for one who longs for liberation to inquire into the nature of categories* (tattvas)*?*

Just as one who wants to throw away garbage has no need to analyse it and see what it is, so one who wants to know the Self has no need to count the number of categories or inquire into their characteristics; what he has to do is to reject altogether the categories that hide the Self. The world should be considered like a dream.

22. *Is there no difference between waking and dream?*

Waking is long and dream short; other than this there is no difference. Just as waking happenings seem real while awake, so do those in a dream while dreaming. In dream the mind takes on another body. In both waking and dream states thoughts, names and forms occur simultaneously.

23. *Is it any use reading books for those who long for liberation?*

All the texts say that in order to gain liberation one should render the mind quiescent; therefore their conclusive teaching is that the mind should be rendered quiescent; once this has been understood there is no need for endless reading. In order to quieten the mind one has only to inquire within oneself what one's Self is; how could this search be done in books? One should know one's Self with one's own eye of wisdom. The Self is within the five sheaths; but books are outside them. Since the Self has to be inquired into by discarding the five sheaths, it is futile to search for it in books. There will come a time when one will have to forget all that one has learned.

24. *What is happiness?*

Happiness is the very nature of the Self; happiness and the Self are not different. There is no happiness in any object of the world. We imagine through our ignorance that we derive happiness from objects. When the mind goes out, it experiences misery. In truth, when its desires are fulfilled, it returns to its own place and enjoys the happiness that is the Self. Similarly, in the states of sleep, *samadhi* and fainting, and when the object desired is obtained or the object disliked is removed, the mind becomes inward-turned, and enjoys pure Self-Happiness. Thus the mind moves without rest alternately going out of the Self and returning to it. Under the tree the shade is pleasant; out in the open the heat is scorching. A person who has been going about in the sun feels cool when he reaches the shade. Someone who keeps on going from the shade into the sun and then back into the shade is a fool. A wise man stays permanently in the shade. Similarly, the mind of the one who knows the truth does not leave *Brahman*. The mind of the ignorant, on the contrary, revolves in the world, feeling miserable, and for a little time returns to *Brahman* to experience happiness. In fact, what is called the world is only thought. When the world disappears, i.e., when there is no thought, the mind experiences happiness; and when the world appears, it goes through misery.

25. *What is wisdom-insight* (jnana drishti)?

Remaining quiet is what is called wisdom-insight. To remain quiet is to resolve the mind in the Self. Telepathy, knowing past, present and future happenings and clairvoyance do not constitute wisdom-insight.

26. What is the relation between desirelessness and wisdom?

Desirelessness is wisdom. The two are not different; they are the same. Desirelessness is refraining from turning the mind towards any object. Wisdom means the appearance of no object. In other words, not seeking what is other than the Self is detachment or desirelessness; not leaving the Self is wisdom.

27. What is the difference between inquiry and meditation?

Inquiry consists in retaining the mind in the Self. Meditation consists in thinking that one's self is *Brahman*, Existence-Consciousness-Bliss.

28. What is liberation?

Inquiring into the nature of one's self that is in bondage, and realising one's true nature is liberation.

Sri Ramana Maharshi

Made in the USA
Monee, IL
05 May 2024